SO-ACM-722

Rookie
Read-About® Health

Where Does Your Food Go?

By Wiley Blevins

Consultants
Nanci R. Vargus, Ed.D.
Assistant Professor of Literacy
University of Indianapolis, Indianapolis, Indiana

Jayne Waddell, MA, RN, LPC
School Nurse, Health Educator, Counselor

Children's Press®
A Division of Scholastic Inc.
New York   Toronto   London   Auckland   Sydney
Mexico City   New Delhi   Hong Kong
Danbury, Connecticut

Designer: Herman Adler Design
Photo Researcher: Caroline Anderson
The illustration on the cover shows a simple view of the digestive system.

Library of Congress Cataloging–in–Publication Data

Blevins, Wiley.
  Where does your food go? / by Wiley Blevins.
      p. cm. – (Rookie read-about health)
Includes index.
Summary: Provides a simple introduction to how the digestive system
works.
  ISBN 0–516–25860–5 (lib. bdg.)   0–516–27854–1 (pbk.)
  1. Digestion–Juvenile literature. [1. Digestion. 2. Digestive
system.] I. Title. II. Series.
  QP145.B56 2003
  612.3—dc21
                                        2003000503

When you eat, your food goes on a journey.

The journey begins with the first bite.

From your first bite, your food travels to every part of your digestive (dye-JESS-tiv) system.

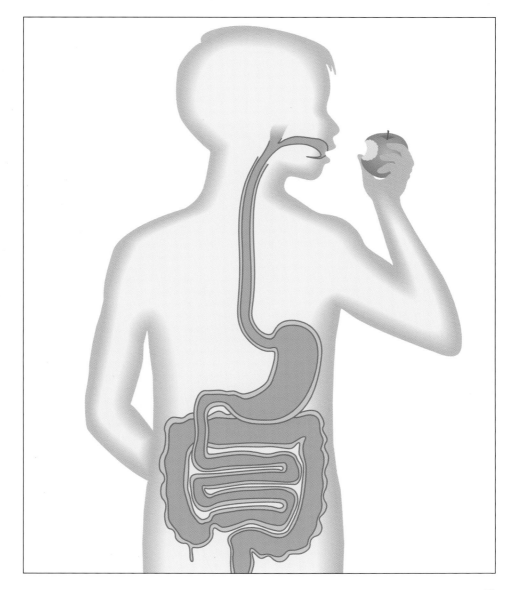

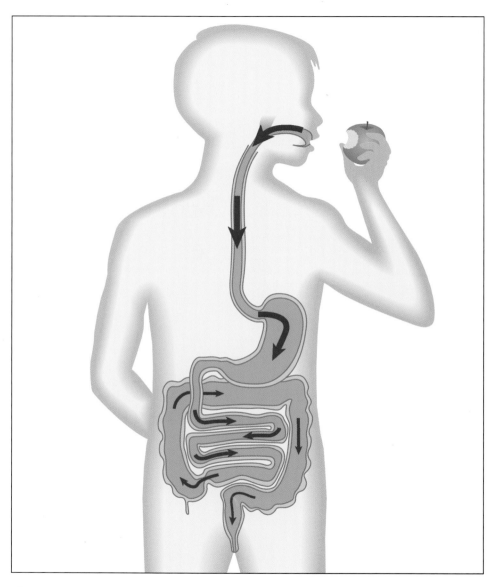

6

To digest means to break into smaller pieces. As your food travels through your body, it is broken into smaller pieces.

Your body uses these pieces of food for energy. Your body needs energy to stay alive.

Crunch. You take a bite of an apple. Your teeth grind the food as you chew.

A special liquid in the mouth, called saliva (suh-LYE-vuh), softens the food.

Saliva has chemicals in it that help break down food.

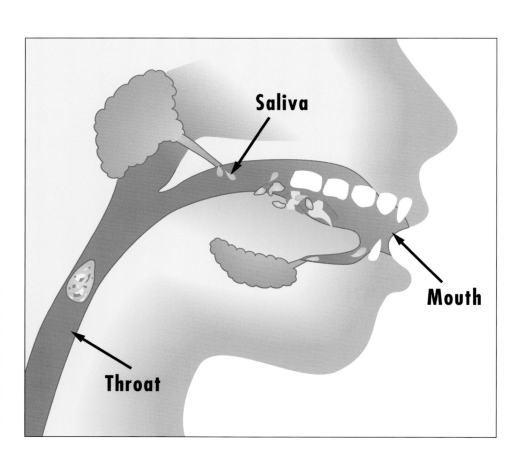

Saliva

Mouth

Throat

10

Now the food is broken
into smaller and softer
pieces. It is ready to
be swallowed.

Gulp!

When you swallow, the bits of apple travel down your body.

First, they go through the esophagus (i-SOF-uh-gus). This is a tube that connects your throat to your stomach.

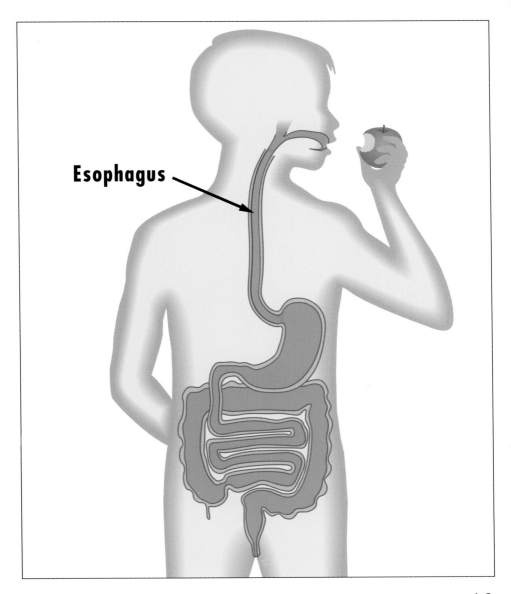

Esophagus

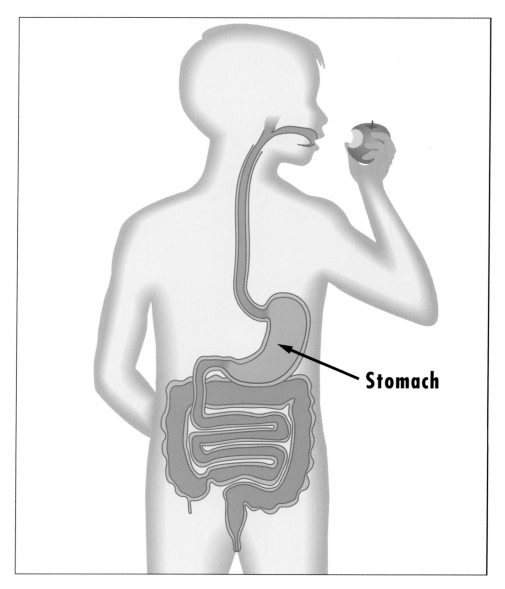

Stomach

Plop!

The bits of apple land in the stomach.

The stomach is like a small bag. It is made of muscles.

The stomach has special juices in it. The muscles mix these juices with the food. The food turns into a thick liquid.

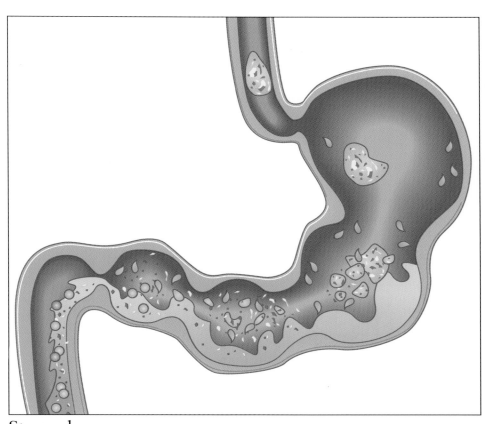

Stomach

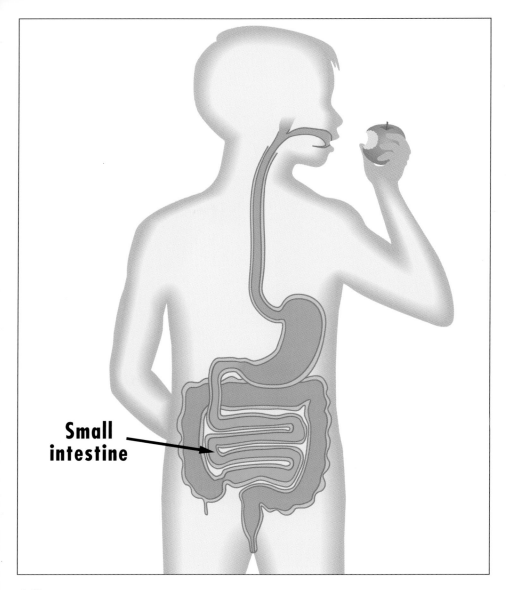

Small intestine

Then, the stomach muscles squeeze the thick liquid into the small intestine (in-TESS-tin).

The small intestine is a long, thin tube. It can be more than 20 feet (6m) long!

The small intestine has an important job to do. It must finish digesting the food.

Here, the thick liquid is turned into a watery liquid.

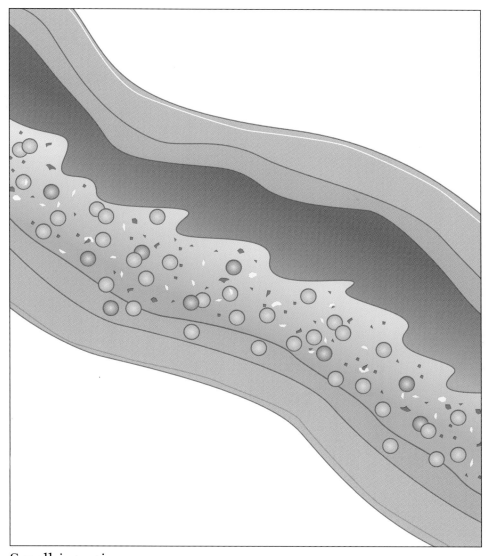

Small intestine

Food has nutrients (NOO-tree-uhnts) in it. Nutrients help you grow.

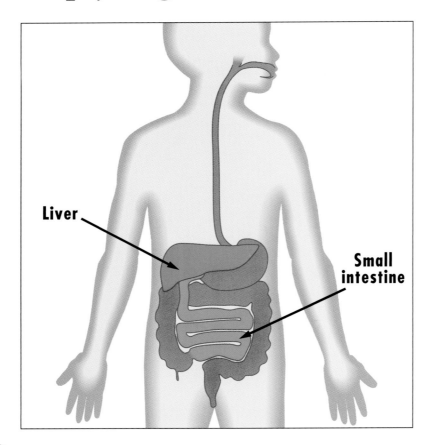

Liver

Small intestine

These nutrients pass through the walls of the small intestine and into blood vessels.

The blood vessels carry these nutrients to the liver. The liver sends them to all parts of your body.

Some parts of food cannot be broken into smaller pieces.

This food is called waste. Waste moves into the large intestine.

The large intestine is also a long tube made of muscle. It is about 5 feet (1.5 m) long.

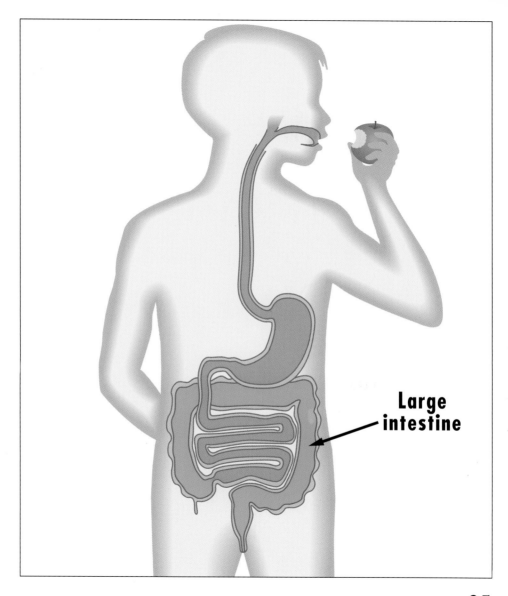

Large intestine

25

GIRLS

GIRLS'
BATHROOM

26

Solid waste is pushed through the large intestine. It is sent out of the body when it reaches the end.

This happens when you go to the bathroom and have a bowel movement.

What an amazing journey your food takes!

29

Words You Know

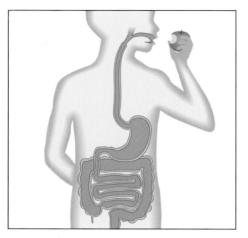

digestive system

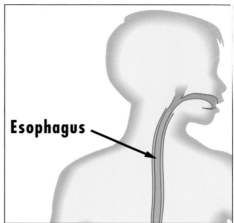

esophagus

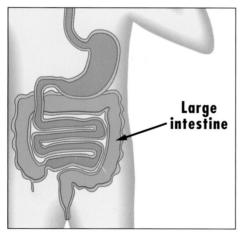

large intestine

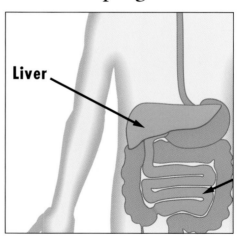

liver

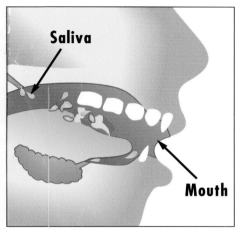

saliva

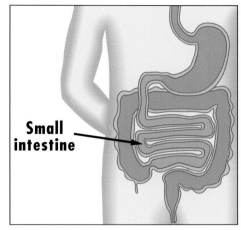

small intestine

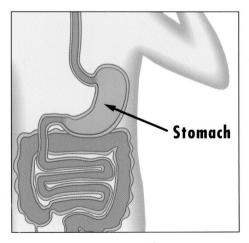

stomach

Index

About the Author

Wiley Blevins is a writer living in New York City. He has written books about other nonfiction topics such as Egypt, slavery, music, and food.

Photo Credits

Photographs © 2003: Ellen B. Senisi: 8, 26, 29, 31 top left; PhotoEdit/ Michael Newman: 3, 28.

Illustrations by Bob Italiano

J
612.   Blevins, Wiley   ood
3   Where Does Your
BLE   Food Go?

$19.50

	DATE		

1/09-4
11/15-57/15

AUG 2 5 2004

BAKER & TAYLOR